UNIQUE SELF
TEST

MICHAEL WELLS

© 2005 by Michael Wells
Text and Illustrations ©1998 by Abiding Life Ministries International

Second printing, 2015

Published by Abiding Life Press
A division of Abiding Life Ministries International
P.O. Box 620998, Littleton, CO 80162

Printed in the United States of America

Library of Congress Cataloging-in-Publication Data
Wells, Michael, 1952–2011
    Unique Self Profile Test / Michael Wells

    ISBN-13: 978-0-9670843-4-3
    1. Christian Psychological Testing

Abiding Life Press

UNIQUE SELF

"For you created my inmost being; you knit me together in my mother's womb"—Psalm 139:13 NIV.

The unique self consists of your inmost being, that part of you that possesses the personality, temperament, talents, abilities, and intellect solely yours at conception. The unique self is given by God before birth and begins to manifest itself shortly after birth; its seat is the soul.

"Then the Lord God formed man of dust from the ground, and breathed into his nostrils the breath of life; and man became a living being"—Genesis 2:7.

As you examine the diagram below, you will notice three concentric circles representing the three elements of man's being: spirit, soul, and body (see I Thessalonians 5:23).

Man's body was formed from the dust of the earth; God breathed His Spirit into man, and this created the soul.

Immediately man began to think, feel, and choose, since the soul is the center of operation for the mind, will, and emotions. Thus the soul became the mediator between the spirit and the body of man. Through the soul man can express what he possesses within; every fruit of the spirit can be manifested through mind, will, and emotions. The soul is analogous to a prism, every one of which, though different, exists for the purpose of receiving and displaying light. The soul of man is the mechanism whereby the light or the darkness within is displayed.

It must be noted that in creating the soul of man, God shows no partiality. To illustrate, we might say God gives every human ten units total of mind, will, and emotion (see the diagram below).

Mind	8	1	1
Will	1	8	1
Emotion	1	1	8
	10	10	10

Some receive 8 units of mind, 1 of will, and 1 of emotion. A child of this type is often exalted because of his great intellect. However, another child may only have 3 units of mind, 2 of will, and 5 units of emotion. This child may not excel in school but does in his God-given ability to care genuinely for others and show empathy. The main point to remember is that no matter what combination of mind, will, and emotion God endows upon an individual, there must be no boasting, bemoaning, or comparing, for God has made each individual solely for the purpose of receiving and displaying His light.

Why not four Basic Temperaments?

The study of man's uniqueness (i.e., temperament, personality, or unique self) is nothing new. Hippocrates, the physician who lived between 470 and 377 B.C., is considered by many to be the father of temperament study. It was he who categorized temperaments into four primary groups: melancholy, phlegmatic, sanguine, and choleric. These classifications were determined as he examined the predominant colors of body fluids in his subjects. However, Hippocrates did not originate the fourfold theory, since the Greek system of thought already embraced four types of personalities represented by summer, winter, spring, and fall. Each of these four were divided into 3 blends, thus furnishing the 12 natures used when astrology was born. Though Hippocrates' approach is far less than scientific or Biblical, he did discover what every mother already knew: Each child is born unique, with a one-of-a-kind view of the world around him and his own approach to relating to others.

The Unique Self Test is a Biblical temperament test using a scriptural model of man for its assessments. Therefore, the traditional four classifications of temperament have been dropped and replaced with the three functions of the soul: mind, will, and emotions. Jesus, commenting on His ability to provide everything man needs, stated He was the way (for the Doer/Will), the truth (for the Thinker/Mind), and the life (for the Feeler/Emotions). Jesus therefore meets the need of every personality type or combination thereof.

Confusing Gifts With UNIQUE SELF

Often the unique self is confused with spiritual gifts, because the majority of tests designed to help Christians know their spiritual gifts simply determine temperament. The strong-willed person, or the "doer," will most often be pinpointed by the rest as a prophet, the emotional person will be revealed as an evangelist, and so on. Please note that God gives the gifts as He wills, and no gift is hindered or accentuated by the natural bent of the unique self. In the Kingdom of God a "doer" can have the gift of service, and a "thinker" can possess the gift of prophecy. One major shortcoming of a test of spiritual gifts is the fact that unbelievers can take the test and be shown as having spiritual gifts!

Understanding the UNIQUE SELF

Understanding unique self is important because the believer is commanded in Luke 9:23 to take up the cross and deny self. The self that is to be denied must be rightly defined, or we may find ourselves trying to deny what God has uniquely made us to be and thus causing a great conflict within.

The Three Selves of Scripture

Three different references to self appear in Scripture; distinguishing between the three facilitates understanding of which one is to be crucified with Christ, which one denied, and finally, which one loved.

As previously mentioned, the unique self is that part of a person formed in the womb (Psalm 139). God is not in the cookie-cutting business, making every human alike. He makes us unique individuals, and although we all have the same purpose in life—which is to fellowship with Him—we will all, as singular creations, express that fellowship in different ways. Unique self is defined as that which is distinctive about each person, including one's God-given talents, abilities, intellect, personality, and temperament.

In some ways the unique self can be thought of as a tool which can do nothing on its own but derives its value from how and by whom it is used. For example, a hammer is a hammer, distinguished only by who uses it and what is accomplished by it; it could be used by a madman to kill someone or by a generous man to build a widow a home. The unique self is used by the Adam-life to produce self-centeredness; by sin, Satan, and the world to construct carnal behavior; or by the very life of Christ to express the Kingdom of God. The unique self cannot be changed, but its source and purpose can be exchanged.

SELF #1   Has to be
• Old Man   Crucified
• Old Nature
• Old Life

Live in Hell
Go to Hell

Talent
Ability
Interests

Unique Self

Express
Flesh

Self #1, then, is the unique self under the control of Adam-life; this self belongs to the unbeliever, or unregenerate man, producing a condition called flesh. A man may possess the God-given ability to start businesses by motivating and persuading others to follow. However, with the old nature in control, the talent and ability that were created to express God instead reveal a condition of flesh, and the man may open a chain of adult bookstores. He has distorted God's gift of unique self and used it for sin, pleasure, and his own purposes.

Many times we see a person whose unique self has been distorted by past events and the ways he has coped with those painful experiences. For example, one's unique self may be characterized as amiable and full of love and concern, and yet under the control of the previously hurt Adam-life it may have learned to behave in a hard and unfeeling manner.

God's command concerning this Self #1 is that it be crucified (Galatians 2:20). The source driving the unique self is what needs to die, not the actual unique self. Self #1 has a course set in one direction, and it follows every signpost which leads it that way. Its destination is hell.

Self #2 is the unique self under the control of the baggage and residue of the dead and removed Adam-life and the unholy trinity, Satan, world, and sin. This person is a born-again believer in a carnal condition. He might use all of the God-given abilities to start a ministry or business that will be for his own glory, financial security, and selfish use. This person is assured of going to heaven, but will continue to experience hell on earth, the continued bondage to sin, Satan, the world, and the past! The command regarding this self is to deny it daily (Luke 9:23) by the power of the cross.

I Die Daily

SELF #2
· Baggage File

Live in Hell
Go to Heaven

Talent
Ability
Interests

Unique Self

Express
Flesh

Self #3 is very important because it is the unique self under the control of Christ's life within. The man in this state enters into the fullness of his being. All of his God-given talents, abilities, intellect, personality, and temperament function properly as they should, and he manifests a condition called walking in the Spirit. Whatever work the man does, Christ does through him, and he is a blessing to all. When Christ controls the unique self, the boundary between spiritual work and secular work disappears, for all labor is spiritual and of Christ. It does not bother this one to perform what some consider to be menial tasks, because Christ is the source. God's perspective of a valuable work is quite different from man's. How many of us think of meeting another's small physical need as highly commendable? "And whoever in the name of a disciple gives to one of these little ones even a cup of cold water to drink, truly I say to you he shall not lose his reward" (Matthew 10:42).

Love Self

SELF #3
• Christ's Life

Live in Heaven
Go to Heaven

Talent
Ability
Interests

Unique Self

Express
Spirit

The commandment concerning Self #3 is that we are to love it (Matthew 19:19). " . . . you shall love your neighbor as yourself."

Failure to distinguish between the three selves will confuse efforts to submit to having self crucified, denying self, and at the same time loving ourselves. The discourse above can serve to clarify the differences.

Love of the unique self as it submits to the Spirit's rule, or Self #3, should be examined further. Until one enters into love of his own unique self, his heart cannot open very widely to others. We live in a culture that extols ability, appearance, and intellect. Any of the fortunate ones who possess these in abundance receive the clear message that they are superior. Paul tries to address the error of this thinking in I Corinthians 12 – 14. God chooses and makes each individual differently according to His purposes. From God's perspective there is really no reason for any of His creatures to exalt themselves above others. Should a man with twenty million dollars feel superior to the poor man when the Lord owns everything? Can a man with an I.Q. of 160 lord it over the man whose I.Q. is 70, when God's immeasurable I.Q. is infinitely well over a trillion? Is the beauty queen as gorgeous to the Lord as the 85-year-old gentle and quiet lady who has walked with Him devotedly for most of her years? We are so foolish and vain! But scriptural insight will not undo what the world continues to say and flaunt.

A Closer Look at the UNIQUE SELF

When I disciple one critical of others, I will immediately ask the question, "What is it about yourself that you do not like?" Perhaps the person feels he is not as intelligent as his friends or not as attractive or talented. Since he does not love what he is, he must tear everyone else down, finding flaws to ease his own feelings of inferiority.

We are to love our neighbors as we love ourselves. If that is true then most neighbors are in for a lot of disappointment when it comes to being loved. Those who possess great talent or ability in a particular area tend to build inferiority in those who cannot function equally well. For example, most evangelists are by creation in their unique selves very outgoing and forceful; if they were not evangelists, they could be car salesmen. They come to the church and tell one story after another about their boldness for the Lord, covertly condemning as ashamed of the Gospel any who are not so forward in their faith but who may simply be those unique selves not suited to going door to door and more competent in such things as following up on any who are interested in pursuing a relationship with Christ. The evangelists who thus condemn do not understand that God makes every member of the body for a different use (the "some sow and some reap" principle); therefore, they continue to exult in their abilities, proclaiming loudly the message that they live the successful (success being that which they do) Christian life naturally. Unfortunately, when someone with this particular unique self pastors a church, he will often develop approaches that center around his natural abilities, not those of the congregation. He then finds himself having to force people to participate. As a result, the programs are usually short-lived. If he could understand the variety of truly distinctive selves the Lord has made, the man would be much more useful as a leader.

A great selection of unique selves exist in the body of Christ, from those who love variety to those partial to detail work, from those following some plan to those devising the scheme of things, those who love adventure and new ideas to those preferring consistency, those working with people and those dealing with things. All who are expressing the nature of their unique selves under the control of Christ's life are a great blessing.

It is important to discern between the three selves, the one cruci-fied, the one to deny, and the one to be loved. The baggage from our old life must be understood as self #2 in order to be readily recognized and denied. Otherwise we might try to deny our unique selves designed by God, an uncomfortable and unproductive thing to do.

Let me ask you, do you love yourself? You should! It may take some time to become pleased with what God has made you to be, but once you do, you will stop comparing yourself with others and begin to appreciate the rest of the body of Christ.

I once asked a man who was a millionaire how he became one. He said it was quite simple; he subcontracted his weaknesses. That is, he surrounded himself not with people who were exactly like him, but with those who were much different in their thinking and attitudes. This promoted much disagreement, but he kept going to the bank with more and more money. Many want to avoid conflict and so surround themselves with people who think exactly like them, but they are never very productive. The body of Christ is prolific because of its diversity, not from attempts to mold everyone into the same type of unique self.

Many believers are easily had; they like people so much that they allow others to use them. God can utilize that distinguishing feature of their unique self in that they never give up on anyone and can stick it out to see the Lord turn someone from defeat to victory. On the other hand, recognizing this characteristic should cause them to enlist the aid of their brothers and sisters who do not have this trait when making decisions.

In I Samuel, Chapter 30, David and his men were involved in a supernatural victory. Those who had been too tired to go to the battle were instructed to remain and keep guard over the baggage. Upon returning from the battle, some "wicked men" did not want to share the spoil with those who chose to stay back rather than fight. David's response was a strong no, for those who protected the baggage were worthy of as much spoil as those who fought. David did not forget that the victory really belonged to God, and after all, what is the purpose of going out to war to gain more if the possibility exists of losing what is already possessed?

There are those of us God puts on the front lines to participate in His supernatural working—never to be viewed as our work—and those of us God has placed to care for what is already possessed; all will receive the same reward. God creates those with great talent, ability, and intellect; no one creates himself. Therefore, boasting must not be in our unique selves, but rather in God.

We hear the parent boasting of the intellect, sports ability, or appearance of his child. Where is God in such boasting and exalting one above the other? Partiality and carnality are shown! Boasting is not good, but is anti-Christ.

There are those Christians who set themselves apart by such things as titles. I have often wondered about the day we stand before the Lord to receive a name that no one else knows. If we used an earthly title to receive glory in life, will the Lord give a name which reflects our selfish desires?

You see, talent, ability, and intellect are relative. Each unique self has its own purpose and usefulness (read I Corinthians 12). We have different gifts, workings, manifestations, bodies, and nationalities, but the same Spirit. Each of us is a different individual, and yet we are all one; together we experience wholeness. Paul encouraged those who are not content with their unique selves (and therefore judge God, their Creator) to love what they are, but at the same time not to seek personal glory from the way God has made them.

Practical Importance of Understanding the UNIQUE SELF

When we enter into a relationship, whether with a mate, a friend, or a co-worker, we begin it at a point of oneness. Each person in the union brings along two bags, one containing belongings from the past (hurts, rejections, perceptions, and subjectivity), and the other bag bearing the unique self. Immediately we can see that between the four bags exists the possibility of conflict.

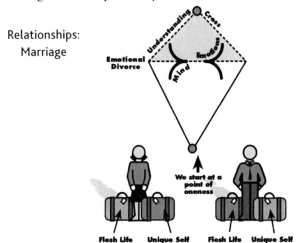

Relationships:
Marriage

Understanding · Cross

Emotional Divorce · Emotions

Mind

We start at a point of oneness

Flesh Life   Unique Self   Flesh Life   Unique Self

Let me illustrate. A woman might enter a marriage with feelings of insecurity and inadequacy stemming from being compared with her more talented and intellectual sister. She carries in the other bag her unique self, that of a thinker. Her husband may be entering the marriage with a bagful of bad experiences with women—beginning with his mother, who still tries to control him—and the only methods he has successfully used to cope (such as avoidance). In his unique-self bag lies a doer. After several years of marriage, the contents of these differing bags begin to collide. Both spouses constantly look for messages that will confirm their assessments of their partner. Everything he does, when perceived through her grid of emotion, seems to prove to her that she does not matter in the relationship, while everything she does convinces him that women, even his wife, try to control him and are to be avoided. The gap in the relationship begins to widen until it reaches a point of emotional divorce, the phenomenon of having emotions run to divorce while the mind refuses to follow. This causes great conflict, so intellectual justifications of their emotions must be sought.

At this point there are two things that could resolve the conflict: understanding and the cross. Through understanding of his wife's unique self and legitimate needs, such as the fact that as a thinker her heart feels she is loved when something special is done for her, he could begin to show affection through means that appear small and insignificant to him. She can recognize his unique self as a doer—with the need for freedom from control—who expresses his love through major events; his most valued commodity is time, the giving of which can be equated to his deeming the recipient as important. We can see that these types of understandings could begin to narrow the gap. However, something is missing, and that is the operation of the cross.

The question must be asked of her, "Let's assume your husband was telling you through his behavior that you are worthless. Where in the Bible is your response of anger, withdrawal, and frustration justified?" The question to him, in turn, would be, "Let's assume your wife is communicating that she wants to control you because you can do nothing right and you are a failure as a husband. Where in the Scriptures is your attitude of avoidance and lack of love justified?" The Bible will not affirm the responses in either case.

Yes, we should understand the unique selves of others; however, we are without excuse if we refuse to deny ourselves and love. In a relationship, understanding of the unique self is valuable, but taking up the cross and denying self is indispensable. The cross which brings self-denial, the freedom afforded others to offend us, and love of our brothers can bring happiness, joy, and fruit even if we never understand the unique self.

As the cross is taken up and understanding is applied, we will see the relationship move back to a point of oneness.

The UNIQUE SELF
as the Body of Christ

Usually the first part of a person noticed is the physical; nevertheless, this is the one aspect of mankind with relatively little value. Though appearance often ignites boasting, it has no true and lasting worth. Scripture speaks to this deception: "Charm is deceitful and beauty is vain" (Proverbs 31:30). In our culture today, since beauty is exalted and coveted, the comely one who is not founded in Christ will too often be used, resulting in suffering and abuse. We know that Jesus Himself did not possess an outer attraction. "He has no stately form or majesty that we should look upon Him, nor appearance that we should be attracted to Him" (Isaiah 53:2). Paul, illustrating the unique self through the analogy of the body, does not make reference to outward beauty; we can conclude that outer appearance does not constitute the unique self.

How can I discern my own unique self? (Remember, the unique self is compared to a hammer, neither good nor bad. The real issue will always be who is controlling it.) The best understanding comes from Paul's analogy of the body as recorded in I Corinthians 12.

There are countless parts and functions of the Body which work together to manifest Christ; but for our purposes we will look at a few representative categories into which members of the Body of Christ can fall: the Thinker, the Doer, and the Feeler.

THE DOER

Looking to our own bodies, we sense that certain members are more important. As a child I saw people missing a limb and would be struck with fear at the thought of ever losing an arm or leg. In my immaturity, I considered the most obvious members to be the most important. Our arms and legs give us strength and allow us to grasp that which is seen. Strength allows us  to achieve what is desired and to move as we see fit. Hence, there are those in the body of Christ who possess great endurance; they are Doers, who see what is needed and go after it. They are likened to the physical muscles; these power members are most needed in the beginning of Christian work, for they are starters. They see no obstacles, they move ahead, and they motivate others to accomplish goals. Just as our physical muscles enjoy exercise and variety, so do these special members of the Body of Christ. No matter how adverse the circumstances, they will see a way clear to minister and increase the Kingdom of God. Opposition and challenge are welcomed; they do not become discouraged with such things, for because of the fortitude that is theirs by nature, they see no hindrances. They are a great blessing to the Body unless the unique self is not under the rule of the Spirit; then they can discourage others on whom they force their wills. They refuse to wait on God and take what seems good to them, for they possess great personal strength. They make others succumb to their desires, listening to no one, bullying and pushing others out of their way to achieve what appeals to them. Because they possess sheer strength of character, they will over-inflate their importance and value to the Body. They are only concerned for others as long as those are perceived to be supportive of them in the new venture of the day. There is nothing worse than a muscle consumed with being one, doing nothing but exercising its force in disregard of the other members. Just as overworking muscles will cause the physical body discomfort, pain, and even sleepless nights, so the Body of Christ often suffers from muscles not under the rule of the Spirit.

THE THINKER

My favorite parts of the body are the ones that cannot be seen; the internal organs in a quiet, unnoticed way monitor and keep the whole body functioning. The heart, liver, lungs, and kidneys are such unseen blessings. Oh, the wonder of these silent, unperceived internal parts! It only takes an instant to fertilize an egg, which would die if not for the hidden work of these inner components, working together to produce the new life that is a baby!

There is a story of a man who lived for many years after having 85% of his spine removed. How? His internal organs were stronger than his outer muscles. A leg can be lost without loss of life, but losing the function of the internal organs brings death.

Those people who function as internal organs, Thinkers, are the most valuable to the growing church. We know that every business, family, and ministry succeeds because of attention to detail. Thinkers are the detail people, the perfectionists, who arrive early, plan the activities, make sure the missionaries, homeless, and hungry are taken care of; in short, they are those who make it all happen. They rarely draw attention to themselves as do muscles, and yet without them the church could not grow. It is unfortunate that because these are hidden members, they receive very little acknowledgment of their importance. Instead they are often led to believe that because they cannot move people with a word, they are not particularly valuable.

I once read that in a certain church no one could be a member if he had not led someone to the Lord. This law, no doubt, was made by a muscle, who would have the tendency to make qualifying rules most easily kept by muscles. This type of tenet would cause considerable consternation for an internal organ, whose created unique self works in quiet, unnoticed ways, and who would find it very unpleasant to have to go door to door arguing and debating the existence of God in hopes of finding a convert.

We must all see our place in the body, recognize God put us there, and love our unique selves. This particular form of unique self gives attention to standards, is logical, specializes, is a critical thinker, will comply with authority, never wants sudden changes, needs reassurance, and would like others to respond to his efforts.

If you have this type of unique self, be warned that when it is operating as a Self #2, you can become critical, feel worthless, judge others only on the basis of performance, be controlling, and withdraw. You will have a tendency to be a loner, so remember that any organ lying by itself on the floor has no purpose.

THE FEELER

There are also organs of the physical body whose attention is toward what is happening outside the body, the Feelers: the eye, ear, nose, mouth, and skin. These members will often lead the body in the direction it is to go. Functioning by feeling and sensing, they can warn of danger or lead to what is pleasurable and good. The Scripture has much to say about these members. "Taste and see that the Lord is good" (Psalm 34:8); "Hear the word of the Lord" (Isaiah 28:14); and, "It is I Myself; touch Me and see" (Luke 24:39).

Feeler

In the body of Christ, feeling members are needed in the maturing church. They will continually draw attention to relationships both to the Lord and to others; they will sense the spiritual and emotional needs of the flock; they desire harmony, love, and fellowship among the members. Feelers will be slow to give up on the defeated and will continue to forgive, giving others another chance. They see people as more important than accomplishments and relationships more sacred than programs; they are, in short, the encouragers.

The flip side, when they are not under the rule of the Spirit, is that they can quickly become competitive, back-biting, depressed, discouraged, manipulated or manipulative, emotionally high one day and low the next, and slow to act. They will strive for social acceptance and possess the unique ability to let others have their way.

When dealing with feelers in the Body of Christ, realize that they want to be around people (God made them that way); they are ruled by emotion and will often misunderstand what is said to them. They want an occasional hug, harmonious relationships, to be helpful to others, and freedom from control and detail work. Encourage them to have a factual basis for their actions and thereby take a systematic approach to projects; help them to follow through, and do not allow them to be manipulated by, unrealistic in their appraisals of, or lax with others.

As we discern the Body of Christ, we will see there are many blends of unique self which are yet to be mentioned. I trust you will begin to see the value of understanding and appreciating the unique selves you, your mate, your children, and, indeed, the whole family of God possess.

Paul makes the statement that " . . . you who judge practice the same things" (Romans 2:1). We often assume someone is communicating to us what we would be trying to say through similar behavior. This misconception has led to much stress in relationships. When my wife, a thinker, is quiet, she is merely mulling things over. On the other hand, when I, a feeler, am silent, I am angry. I spent several years of my marriage assuming my wife was angry during her quiet times of thinking!

How the different
UNIQUE SELVES respond

There is great strength and value in recognizing the unique selves existing in the Body of Christ, for this discernment allows wisdom to be utilized in employing the service and abilities of each individual member. The illustrations below will help clarify differences in the temperament types.

Example #1

If I were on the bow of a sinking ship, I would want to have with me a muscle member, one who makes quick, directive decisions, for I am quite confident he would inform us we were going to tie the boat oars together with our belts and jump off. I would not want a sensory member with me, for he would only put his arms around me and tearfully tell me he was sorry I would soon be dead! Nor would I want to be accompanied by an internal member, who analyzes everything to death; we simply would not have the time!

Example #2

If I just inherited one million dollars I would not want to talk to a muscle member, who would tell (not ask) me to invest in a cat-skin coat farm (where the cats eat the rats, the rats eat the cats, and we get the coats for nothing) because it seems good to him. I would like to consult the sensory member to find out about the real needs around me. I would also like to talk to an internal member, who could analyze the whole cat-farm proposal and ask crucial questions, such as, "Do people buy cat-skin coats?"

Example #3

Imagine all three unique selves sitting in a restaurant with one additional guest. The guest has just eaten a salad, and a piece of lettuce is stuck between his two front teeth. The Thinker shuts down and fixes his attention on the guest's teeth; he cannot continue his meal, for something is out of place. The Feeler is in emotional turmoil, feeling embarrassed for the guest. However, he will not bring the matter to the person's attention for fear of offending. The Doer, upon noticing the lettuce, might render unsolicited aid by pulling out a pocketknife and reaching forward to dig the lettuce out. If the guest's lip gets cut in the process and he begins to complain, the Doer responds, "That is what bandages are for!"

Example #4

If all three Unique Selves were given the opportunity to receive a vaccination Monday through Friday, the Thinker would choose Friday, giving him plenty of time to think about and prepare for it. The Feeler would want to get his over with right away and not look, while the Doer would give himself the shot!

Example #5

Observing all three at work parking vehicles would be revealing. The Thinker would park exactly between the lines and be frustrated with those who do not. The Feeler would not notice he has parked at an angle to but not within the lines. The Doer would park anywhere he wants: the handicapped parking, employee of the month's space, or the bank president's spot.

Knowing your unique self is simple and does not take prolonged inward vision, so be careful that you do not become obsessed with it, for often such an absorption has self-adulation at its root. Your unique self is determined by those things you do naturally and most comfortably (this is different from the behaviors such as withdrawal, avoidance, and erroneous fears that may develop through false identity messages). This does not refer to any type of sin that may easily ensnare you, but rather to the type of activity to which you find yourself drawn like a magnet. Are you always late getting home because you talk to the gas station attendant or a neighbor? Your unique self is a people person, a sensory member, a Feeler. If you have all the nuts, bolts, and screws in their proper baby-food jars in the garage, then your unique self, a Thinker, has been created to enjoy detail and do a job right. Are you easily bored, anxious to get on to the next project? You are a muscle member, a Doer.

Just remember that however God has made you, enjoy yourself, love yourself, and refuse to listen to those who would intimidate by boasting in their natural abilities. Whatever measure He has

given you, enjoy it. If you are not as intellectual as another, that was
God's decision, and if you complain, you make yourself out to be
the Creator. "Who are you, O man, who answers back to God? The
thing molded will not say to the molder, 'Why did you make me
like this,' will it?" –Romans 9:20. Remember, too, that the gifts
of the Spirit rarely follow our normal traits; they are not the same
as natural abilities, which even an unbeliever possesses, but
are supernatural.

The UNIQUE-SELF Pyramid

Notice at the top of the unique-self pyramid there is a point, or
rather, a dot. This represents the Thinker, who by creation is concerned with the details of life. Because of excessive mental energy,
he focuses or obsesses on one point until it is resolved to his satis-
faction. This causes the Thinker to see the black dot on the white
wall, and thus he can easily spiral into criticism and depression.

For the Thinker, the task equals his identity; that is, he cannot
separate his worth from the task at hand. To criticize the work
of the Thinker is to belittle him. The best animal to symbolize

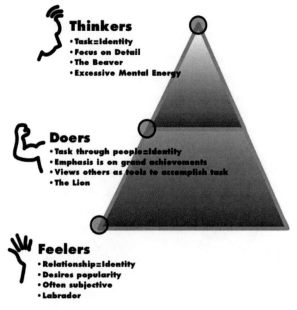

Thinkers
- Task=Identity
- Focus on Detail
- The Beaver
- Excessive Mental Energy

Doers
- Task through people=Identity
- Emphasis is on grand achievements
- Views others as tools to accomplish task
- The Lion

Feelers
- Relationship=Identity
- Desires popularity
- Often subjective
- Labrador

the Thinker is the beaver, who likes to stay in one place and keep everything in order. Thinkers often wish others would follow the rules and act more sensibly.

In the middle of the pyramid is the Doer. Although also task oriented, he uses relationships to accomplish the job. Many will have the feeling that the Doer is using them while unconcerned with their welfare; however, this is not the case. The Doer sees a goal and considers himself to be the hub and others to be the spokes to support him. His foremost concern is with the overall picture of the big wheel that allows the accomplishment of the task. The animal that best exemplifies the Doer is the lion, who dislikes being caged or forced into inactivity. The Doer whose actions are restricted in some way will pace back and forth, biting anyone who gets in his way; he will constantly look for a savior who possesses the key to alleviate the situation. Attention to detail is not a priority for the Doer and can, in fact, be quite annoying. Approaches to spirituality developed by Doers will accentuate those things they can naturally do, such as witness, preach, and be bold. Others unable to perform these things well will struggle and be considered weak. The Doer, though, has an equally difficult time following up on those he shepherds and completing the necessary details of daily ministry.

At the bottom of the pyramid is the Feeler; relationships define his identity, for if they are negative, he will perceive that his self-worth has diminished. His goal in life includes positive relationships and being highly regarded; he is primarily interested in how well he is liked. The Feeler is often highly subjective and sensitive. The animal best illustrating him is the Labrador Retriever, who loves to be included and appreciates overt displays of affection.

UNIQUE-SELF Perceptions

Imagine the Empire State building with a Doer standing at the top and a Thinker at the bottom. The Doer will often consider the Thinker to be passive, because the Thinker must analyze before making a comment. The Thinker will consider the Doer to be domineering and impulsive because of his constant need to initiate action. Now let's also imagine that these two are a married couple.

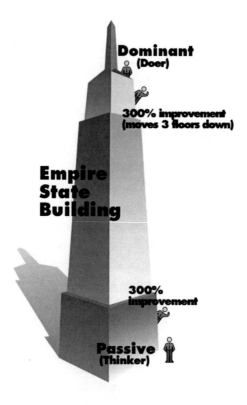

The Doer yells down to the Thinker that he or she needs to be more active and dominant. The desire to please leads the Thinker to attempt to become more active and spontaneous by making a 300% improvement, moving up three floors from the bottom. Does the Thinker look any closer to the Doer despite the great improvement? Not at all! Therefore, the Doer yells down, "Aren't you going to try at all?" The Thinker's efforts are not rewarded, so back to the bottom of the building he or she returns to live more comfortably. On a scale of 1 to 10 in difficulty, moving up three floors was a 10 for the Thinker, but was considered a 1 for the

Doer. This inability of the Doer to get into the shoes of another creates in the Thinker the very thing the Doer despises. Now imagine that the Thinker yells, "Slow down!" to the Doer, who moves down three floors, again a 300% improvement; however, as before, this measure of improvement is not appreciated by the Thinker, who asks if the Doer cares to improve at all. This discourages progress for the Doer, who also in time returns to the zone more comfortable.

We must understand and learn to appreciate the differences in others' unique ways of behaving and communicating love in order to disciple effectively. For instance, often others feel the Thinker does not love because his way of expressing it differs so greatly from their ways. If understood, the Thinker would be seen to have been showing affection in many covert ways, such as with a nice meal, the car's being filled with gas, the appliances' having been repaired, and so on.

Attractions and Annoyances of the UNIQUE SELF

What attracts us to the DOER
- Independence
- Confidence
- Accomplishments

What annoys us about the DOER
- Disregard for feelings of others
- Condemning tone of speech; driving us to do for them
- Explosions
- Egotistical manner

What attracts us to the FEELER
- Makes us feel good
- Caring, loving, kind
- Wants to please

- Enthusiastic
- Impulsive

What annoys us about the FEELER
- Subjectivity (so sensitive and emotional)
- Hogs the conversation
- Manipulates
- Oversells his ideas; excessively enthusiastic

What attracts us to the THINKER
- Serious
- High standards in work
- Highly intelligent
- Often talented in the arts
- Consistent
- Extremely loyal

What annoys us about the THINKER
- Moves too slow
- Does not like taking risks
- Critical; unaffectionate
- Controls through a biting humor

UNIQUE SELF is never an excuse for behavior

We must be reminded that Unique Self is never an excuse for our behavior. Every Unique Self must display the fruit of the Spirit: love, joy, peace, patience, kindness, goodness, faithfulness, gentleness, and self-control. If not, the believer is walking in the flesh.

Energy levels of the UNIQUE SELF

The three primary Unique Selves have differing energy levels, as noted in the diagram. The Thinker's energy starts out high and is drained by the end of the day, the Feeler's energy begins low and ends high, while the Doer's energy begins high and ends high. This is valuable for understanding behaviors and as insight into when might be the best time for dialogue or when would be the most effective time for the enemy to attack.

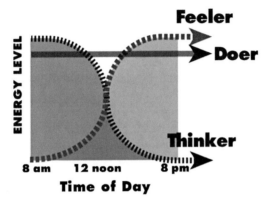

What is normal for you?

Hopefully, understanding your own unique self will enable you to discern what is normal for you.

Again, we are not to disciple another from our own shoes. In fact, there would appear to be a built-in inferiority in our society for the Thinker, since the majority of celebrities are Doers and Feelers who covertly define what is normal for the rest of society. This is most often seen in the church, where the Doer or Feeler defines spirituality by what he or she can accomplish naturally. It is worth noting that over 60% of believers come to Christ slowly and methodically, not knowing the exact date of their conversion. However, the conversion experienced by the minority—an explosion—has been touted as the norm for all.

Individual temperament characteristics

Very few people exhibit compulsive unique selves, those not blended with at least one other type of unique self. Since you understand yourself better than does any test, it will be up to you to decide your own blend.

At the right side of the bar chart on the last page, notice that zero to 100% is displayed. The placement of your score in each of the three areas—Thinker, Feeler, and Doer—will indicate a percentage score from which you will discover roughly how much you contain of each primary unique self. Thus, if you are 80% Thinker, then 80% of the following unique-self traits probably apply to you. Determine which characteristics apply and put a check by them.

THE THINKER
Basic Characteristics

- Values truth and honesty and expects others to value them
- Prefers order
- Tends to look to money for security
- 1 - 3 close friends (extremely loyal)
- Needs quiet time alone each day (people drain his energy)
- Analytical (can get lost in the forest)
- Feelings of inferiority (will not recognize his own talent, ability, and intellect or believe you when you point it out)
- Knows all that is bad about himself (This can allow him to become a blame-taker. For example, the mother who knows she is a bad mother 5% of the time will, when told she has done something wrong, accept blame for being a terrible mother 100% of the time.)
- Perfectionist
- Excessive mental energy
- What he is thinking about determines his mood
- Must have something in mind at all times (often likes to read before going to bed)
- Therefore, he is most often given to anxiety attacks. Having examined himself and found everything wrong within, he is nervous about having such a person in charge. Imagine a woman

on an airplane taking a vacation and finding a note in her purse describing all that is wrong with the person in whose care she left the children. There is no possibility of turning the plane around. What would happen next? Her anxiety would go up. This is what it is like for a perfectionist who knows everything wrong with himself yet finds himself in positions of responsibility.

- Extreme fear of the unknown; tell him ahead of time about your plans
- Typically a late bloomer because of the reluctance to take risks
- High standards, higher than God's
- Keeps lists, even invisible ones
- Internalizes anger and does not have the luxury of daily explosions
- 60% of people have at least half of the above-mentioned characteristics
- It is worth noting that this category of person lends itself most readily to the slow and methodical conversion experience consistent with the need to analyze all data

Misunderstandings

- Cannot separate task from identity and will think you are attacking him when questioning the task
- Expressions of love are in the little things done for others
- Serious and quiet moods are not to be confused with disapproval; he is usually merely thinking
- Biting humor is often a release of pressure along with the expression of genuine acceptance of the one(s) toward whom it is directed

Under Pressure

- He will withdraw
- Becomes critical of others and himself
- May entertain thoughts of suicide
- Attempts to control the environment and others
- Becomes depressed

- Given to anxiety attacks
- Replays the hurts others have caused him continually in his mind

Affection
- Low to moderate displays of physical expression
- When approached to be held may begin to feel suffocated

Needs
- Security in a situation
- Someone who will promote him and see his value
- Recognition of the impact that his attention to detail has on daily life
- Give him some quiet time alone
- Give him time to adjust before forcing him to act
- Set his mind on the positive, not allowing the negative spiral to worsen

Fears
- Antagonism

In Relationship with God
- Difficulty in forgiving himself or others
- Difficulty in letting go of a mental obsession (it has so filled his life, what will he do without it?)
- The fear God will not act or will make him do something that is not sensible
- Accepts forgiveness
- Failure may be a ten for him, but a one for God, since his standards are too high
- Wants to understand before believing
- Equates hearing God with intellectual insight

Value in the Kingdom
- He does the work
- Extremely loyal
- Good teacher

- Great discipler (one-on-one)
- Critical analyses help keep the church in check
- Will not deviate from the teaching received

Vocations

- Quality detailed work
- Can work with others if they are competent
- More satisfied if with responsibility he has authority
- A consistent job description, not one that is continually changing
- He wants to work and then go home with minimal work infringement on his personal life

THE FEELER
Basic Characteristics

- Relationships = Identity
- Highly subjective (often saying, "I didn't say that"); everything read through a grid of emotion
- Will pout when rejected
- Will often follow the morals of the crowd
- Life is a party
- When a guest enters the home, the guest is made to feel important and the family can get left out
- Will allow others to fail him
- Short memory when it comes to the faults of others
- He manipulates to allow you to have his way
- Extremely sensitive to the needs of others
- Can empathize easily
- People pleaser
- Reject him and he will reject you back
- Moment-by-moment explosions
- His conversion is often the explosive type
- Motivational
- Enthusiastic
- Desires popularity (not all do, you know)

- Freedom of expression
- Can easily verbalize feelings

Misunderstandings

- Oversells you on anything
- Reacts to a person, not the facts
- When others enter a room, you can feel he has cast you aside
- Becomes overcommitted due to his desire to be a people pleaser

Under Pressure

- Becomes sulky
- Will physically reject you; because physical rejection hurts him, he assumes it will likewise hurt you
- Becomes very subjective
- Accepts blame and withdraws from others into himself
- Becomes depressed if relationships are bad

In Affection

- Hug him a hundred times and he wants one more
- Nearly impossible to meet his physical need for affection
- Give him a hug each time you pass by, for receiving affection raises his self-esteem

Needs

- Plenty of activities with others
- After he is completely drained, he will withdraw to rest
- Must be constrained to concentrate on the task and the facts
- Give him the opportunity to do something special
- Time = love

Fears

- Complex relationships
- Pressuring people
- Feeling that he has harmed others
- A fixed environment

Relationship with God

- A constant feeling of rejection
- A Feeler must learn to live out of the fact, not the feeling, of who God is; emotions often must be rejected
- He must see that it is possible to have a deep relationship with God, so that he does not allow other people to crowd out God's importance
- Wants to run from God when there has been a failure
- Wants to feel God before believing
- Equates God's presence with feelings

Value to the Kingdom

- In touch with the hurts, needs, and feelings of others
- Since the majority of believers act from fact, not feeling, input from the Feeler helps keep the heart in the outlook and direction of the ministry
- He will see the good in others and desire to give them one more chance
- He has the ability to encourage and enjoys that role
- He leads through persuasion, believing things will get better

Vocation

- Any people-intensive job
- Selling, management, or the people-helping professions
- He will need variety and change

THE DOER
Basic Characteristics

- Strong-willed
- Accomplishing the task through people
- Projects a sense of confidence and independence
- Enjoys glory stories wherein he is the hero
- Cannot see obstacles

- Has a tendency to distort reality to fit his present goals
- Lots of irons in the fire
- Inconsistent
- Hates to be confused by the facts
- Has immediate explosions that knock everyone to the ground and then wonders why they don't get up more quickly
- Enjoys a challenge, even if it is a problem he has created
- Easily bored
- Out of touch with the feelings of others
- He often thinks of himself in the third person: "Ed built this . . ."
- Has no qualms throwing a parade for himself complete with banners
- Extremely energetic
- Extremely creative
- Others are viewed as a tool to be used until broken
- Easily accepts aggression
- Enjoys a good fight

Misunderstandings

- When unable to accomplish a goal, others are blamed
- Though he disregards your feelings, he is not disregarding you; he values loyalty
- Often his perceived harsh responses are attempts to control in order to accomplish the goal
- He is frustrated with lack of progress, though it always appears he is frustrated with you
- He cannot be taken as seriously as he takes himself
- When a goal is before him, he honestly has difficulty heeding anyone around him

Under Pressure

- He will feel caged and begin to pace
- Looks for a savior to loosen the restraint and allow him to get on
- Becomes a loner

- Can become belligerent
- Assertive
- Dominant
- Condescending in attitude toward others

Affection
- Outgoing
- Passive-aggressive
- Wants support for the plan of the day
- Physical affection on demand

Needs
- Challenge
- Others who are straightforward (he can take it)
- Variety
- Freedom from controls
- Very little supervision

Fears
- Boredom
- Failure of accomplishing all tasks and goals
- Routine
- Giving control to another

Relationship with God
- Most pliable when broken
- Desires to see the power of God
- Seeks God under extreme pressure
- Equates the work of God with the personal presence of God
- Respects the power of God

Value to the Kingdom
- Initiates changes
- Driver vs. leader
- Is not sidetracked by the complaints of others

- Can stand up under the most vicious attacks
- Accomplishes the goal in spite of obstacles
- Large quantities of this type person are not needed; one can keep many people busy

Vocations
- Jobs that present a challenge
- Jobs that need a vision to be completed
- Henry Ford, Michaelangelo
- Inventors
- Jack-of-all-trades

THE BLENDS

As mentioned before, most individuals are not compulsively Thinkers, Feelers, or Doers; they are generally a combination or blend of two or more temperament types. The blend is determined by the primary and secondary unique-self traits. The primary traits are often softened by the secondary traits. For example, in the Practical blend, the high Thinker would be detail-oriented and would prefer to work alone, but the secondary aspect of Feeler would balance those tendencies by adding a relational element and thus allowing the individual to enjoy being with others and not fixate on the minute details of life.

The number of different blends varies according to how many people exist. We will only examine a sampling of characteristic combinations.

PRACTICAL
Thinker-Feeler

The practical unique self is defined by a simple word, "**steady.**" He is not moved readily by emotion but rather examines the facts and moves toward the goal. The story of the tortoise and the hare might best describe the Practical's approach to life and tasks. Once the goal is agreed upon, others would be hard pressed to find a more

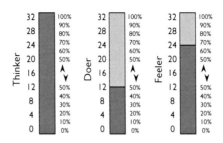

consistent and **loyal** person to put in a team, and he can work
alone or with others, although he can secretly be competitive as
he observes what he judges to be others' stupid decisions. Business
owners would do well to spot the Practical person, elevate his job
status, and give him a task, keeping in mind he desires excellence
and is sensitive to criticism. However, if he perceives that those with
whom he is working are not as good as he, rather than complaining
overtly, he will simply get on with the job. There is an ingrained
fear of change and risk-taking, which can keep the Practical in a
less than satisfying job. He values information, would like to know
what is happening, and wants to **be included** in the decisions
concerning the job, since this is directly attached to the Practical's
security. He **hates complex relationships** and finds security where
people are consistent. Inconsistencies in others at work or in his circle of intimacy will drive him to the brink of frustration, though his
frustration is not immediately vented but builds, like the fire under
a **pressure cooker**, until there is an explosion. The deception is that
the explosion was caused by the most recent event, when actually it
was the culmination of days, weeks, or months of aggravation.

Those married to a Practical will already know that feelings need to
be pried out of him. However, his **loyalty** can never be questioned.
He demonstrates his love through the little tasks, consistency, pro-
vision, working in difficult situations, and more. There is a bit of
an attitude of, "I told you I loved you the day we got married. If anything changes, I will let you know." The Practical will give a lot in
a relationship and covertly expect a lot. He is **full of surprises**. The
child of a Practical will learn that after being told of a mistake, he

will more often than not then be met with a **loving, compassionate, and understanding heart**. The Practical will have a tendency not to act on what he feels but rather to **fantasize** about how he feels, due to the fact that acting out in the mind is safer than actually acting on the feelings. A Practical will sit in a chair, think about dating, wonder what the date would be like, reflect on getting married, ponder having rebellious children, consider the possibility of a divorce, and then get depressed, though he has never even left the chair to have those actual experiences. Under pressure he will stall while he lies in bed, thinking and feeling but not acting. Indecision will cause more damage than a wrong decision. The Practical would be well served to decide today, wait seven days, and then act on the decision.

Generally, the gifting, **talent, abilities**, loyalty, friendship, and knowledge of a Practical are rarely rewarded, although he is the oil that makes the machine in every business, home, and church function properly. He goes about his tasks as a servant and requires very little. Every job and home is the poorer without the Practical, since his ability to **examine**, come up with well thought-out solutions, and show compassion is a great asset. He would like to be included and initiated toward; once he is, what is hidden within can be discovered. The Practical is a Pandora's Boxful of surprises with a wealth of information and interests, all useful. It is unfortunate that he can be plagued by feelings of laziness, perhaps from allowing the high Doer and Feeler to be the model of "normal," and once that is believed, the Practical will struggle with inadequacy. He is not. He is **technical and specialized**.
Biblical Character: John Mark

PERFECTIONIST
Thinker-Doer

For the perfectionist unique self, his task is attached to his personhood, his identity; he puts a little bit of himself in everything he does. Therefore, to question or criticize his task is tantamount to attacking him. A statement such as, "Your endeavor is sub-par," is

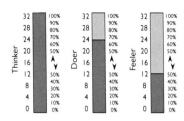

heard as, "You are sub-par." Any subsequent negative observation about his task will elicit a reaction. The Perfectionist has actually seen the **flaws** in his work before the observer did, has punished himself, and merely wants to fix the problem without interference. The parent does not need to dwell on the mistakes of the Perfectionist child, who would have already seen them or needs only a little help recognizing them. Time on his own should be given to allow the child to fix the issue, problem, or task. It is important to remind the Perfectionist child that he is not defined by what he does or what he knows, but rather by other contributions. When praise is received for a job well done, the Perfectionist prefers not to hear that, either. Praise brings its own kind of burden: the bondage to perform and maintain the excellent standard set by his **giftedness.** The Perfectionist must learn that jobs are never completed, but are rather abandoned. In other words, the real money, as it might be said, is in getting a job done at 80% quality, which is 100% to the rest of us. The gifted Perfectionist can easily complete a job to 80% but then labor for weeks to reach an unattainable image of perfection he very subjectively defined as being **100%.** This frustration is the fuel for the Perfectionist's constant **procrastination.** Since in his mind the task will not be perfect, signaling to him he is a failure as a person, he avoids the task until external pressure forces him to work.

Because of tasks' equaling identity, the Perfectionist is not a team player. If forced to work with others, the "others" must be as competent as he is, or he would rather do the job himself. This attitude has led many Perfectionists to exhaustion. **Michelangelo** had many helpers to paint the Sistine Chapel, yet all were dismissed and he did the majority of the work himself, which was eventually a contributing factor to his death. The Perfectionist can be an **excellent doctor, lawyer, innovator, scientist, and more**. If there is any detail work to do, the Perfectionist will do a better job than anyone. What he lacks in peopling skills is more than made up for in his **high standard of work**. He is a self-motivated planner with drive, but he must be **directed**. Give him the information and allow him to make the decision. Pushing him will only cause him to drop anchor, which will lead to his constantly beating himself up over all that could have been done. Given a task, he will **investigate, appraise, and act**. He **does not like to be questioned**, because he does not believe another could possibly have studied the issue as he has or have all of the information. He will follow a leader if—and it is a big if—he believes that the person he is following is better, smarter, and more competent than he is.

The Perfectionist will open up to very few, very seldom. On that odd day, those close to him must take care to listen and hold everything said in the highest confidence. The Perfectionist wants to hear nothing other than the **truth**, which he values highly. He is also looking for a role model that could show how to live in a world full of sloppy people and not go crazy. He is vexed by all injustice and by those who do not see the need to adhere to rules. Under pressure he will have a tendency to become **obsessive** and **withdrawn**; someone must enter the cave, so to speak, and pull him out. Remember, too, that the Perfectionist **fears rejection** and usually is not the initiator of affection. If rejected, he would be crushed, so he will wait for the other to make the first move and remain emotionally safe. Also, all those within his circle of intimacy are seen as an extension of himself; this leads to the constant **examination** of the words, behavior, and dress of those he loves. The Perfectionist can be verbally cutting at his worst and display a wonderfully dry sense of humor at his best.
Biblical Model: The Physician Luke

CREATIVE
Doer-Thinker

The creative unique self has a lot of drive accompanied by his own **high standards** of perfection that are applied not only to himself but to all those in close proximity. Those in the creative person's circle are considered an extension of himself. Therefore, he is equally **hard on himself** and others. His style of leadership is getting behind those that are to accomplish **tasks** and kicking them forward.

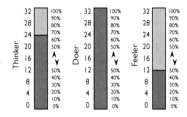

He will tell the truth without sweetening it, for his identity rests in the ability to get others busy accomplishing his plan. Standing in the hub of the moving wheel, with each blink he sees a new spoke, something new he could have others doing. A designer who will maintain control, this person could easily keep many people busy. It is important to understand that his **bluntness** should not be confused with rudeness and that he is as **loyal** as he is blunt. **Truth is of primary importance** for the Creative. If something is borrowed from him and broken, he will be more upset with a lie about breaking it than the fact of its being broken. He is a **risk taker** and actually easily bored when finding himself without a challenge. One married to a Creative might hear, "The only thing wrong with this family is that my advice and directions are not being followed exactly." Remember, too, that the Creative cannot be pushed or pulled, but only **directed**. He wants information and the freedom to choose, with no outside force, the direction in which he has determined to move, and **aggression does not** affect the direction. At this point, one might ask, "What is the value of a creative unique self?" The value is great. For example, on a sinking ship the

Creative **will act with a plan**. "Tie the tables together and make a raft!" This will be done with great haste. Also, once the Creative gets a grasp on a truth, concept, or project, he will hold onto it and not waver, no matter what kind of oppression or obstacles are met. A **self-starter** with a plan, his motto is, "If it is worth doing at all, it is worth doing well." The person married to one will never want for the necessities of life and will most likely fare much better than normal. He is fiercely independent, wants freedom from control, and even when on an impossible path he is frustrated at being told no or told *what cannot be done* and wants to surround himself with those that have an equal zeal for *what can be done*.

Biblical Example: Paul

MOTIVATOR
Doer-Feeler

The unique self of the Motivator is usually well liked, because **he enjoys people** and goes to the extra effort of **including them**, asking them various questions and making them feel as though they have become the center of attention. Within a few minutes it is felt that the Motivator has been a **friend** for a long time. He has the ability to become all things to all men and will engage on several levels on a variety of topics. He is objective and yet takes into account the feelings of those with whom he has surrounded himself.

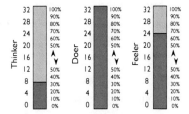

If the Motivator is given to lofty or earthly pursuits, he will find that people follow gladly and enjoy the exciting trip in response to his **air of confidence**, a certain **charm**, a **sense of direction**, and his excitement about his plans. In fact, he **leads by pulling others along** and yet takes a measure of responsibility for the direction he offers. His drive does not allow for a complete release of tasks to another. The Motivator is an apt counselor when it comes to directing others, like a Tom Sawyer letting "**others have his way**." If he believes in a product, he puts forth a nearly **mystical presentation**, the merits of which drive a person to buy without much thought about the product! His **manipulation** can have the goal of enrichment or abuse, and so the Motivator must be careful to use the gained emotional trust for the wellbeing of those he is leading. He can appear bigger than life with his grand accomplishments that appeal to the "Feeler," because of the perceived notoriety, and at the same time discourage the "Thinker," who walks away feeling he is lacking by way of comparison. The Motivator is given to the senses but is not dominated by them. It is crucial that the Motivator surround himself with people, which can cause a backlash of **inward exhaustion** after he has covertly promised to meet too many emotional needs in scores of people. He appears to put himself in places where he must need others and others must need him. The great positive is his **ability to lead**—really lead—by example those who have been swayed by emotion in the wrong direction. The bottom line is that though he needs others, **he does care** for them. Biblical Character: Peter

AMIABLE
Feeler-Thinker

The amiable unique self is an asset to any **team** activity, since he would prefer to perform a task with a group than by himself. Because of the **calming effect** an Amiable has on people, he is jokingly referred to as the Valium of the world. His first and foremost concern when accomplishing a task is the welfare of the

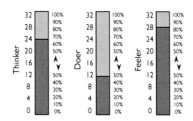

people involved with him. The Amiable has the ability to verbalize, after thinking, what others on the team are feeling. When introducing someone new to a team, the Amiable will **initiate the relationship** and include the new member. He brings an air of refreshment and relationship to what might be considered a mundane job. Being good-natured, **friendly**, and likeable, he is not given to the frustration with a task exhibited by those higher in Thinker. Speech is often deliberate, and he is **not given to reactions** but takes a wait-and-see attitude. He **is not excitable** and is a very good person to have in a crisis. He will come up with a plan while considering the feelings of those around him. Rarely would the Amiable be thought of as a leader, which is a mistake. He is simply not interested in the spotlight, but in his circle of influence it becomes quite obvious that he has the ability to initiate and lead and to inspire others. His style of leadership is to walk with those around him and, through education, create a safe environment in which to facilitate risk-taking and being comfortable with the task at hand. His value in a business is not so much in overproduction but in **building relationships**, often stopping to talk to those for whom he is doing the work. Pushing an Amiable to act or make a decision will certainly backfire, since he prefers to move according to his timetable, not that of others. Therefore, family and friends will experience a level of frustration in what is seen as **inactivity** and the refusal to take a risk, and indeed, he may well need a push when this trait is exhibited. As a child the Amiable is open to abuse by those that see him as weak, inactive, and just too nice. This stems from his being **very loyal** and **afraid to cause emotional harm** to others; thus he develops false loyalty and stays in a relationship much longer than the facts would require. He is slow to anger, and his calm and quiet nature makes for an excellent counselor; he will exude safety and a quiet confidence that things will get better. One danger is allowing the Feeler in him to overwhelm the Thinker, because this will take the form of two manifestations. First, he will suffer with **false guilt**, and second, decisions will be made based on feelings rather than facts. Keep the Amiable away from a slick salesperson, who will feed the emotions until a purchase is made based wholly on what is occurring in the moment. Later there will be regret when the Thinker once again is able to weigh in. A person who is one of the Amiable's one to three close friends will be the beneficiary of a staunch ally even in the face of overt stupidity.

Biblical Type: David

SELLER
Feeler-Doer

The Seller might be called the perfect **second man**. Needed in every organization, the second man becomes the buffer between the employer and the employees, the manufacturer and the purchaser, and the seller and the buyer. His style of leadership actually only encompasses himself, for though gregarious, he is a loner preferring to work alone without any of the confinements that might limit his

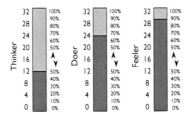

freedom to roam. The Seller **hates confinement**; if put in a position of tedious, repetitive tasks, he will constantly pace and look for a human being with whom to interact. Because of this desire for interaction, the Seller will subconsciously **procrastinate** and then do everything all at once to avoid the perceived boredom from doing the task daily. He purposely puts himself under pressure to be more productive. The wise Seller is willing and able to **delegate the details** of his job and daily life. He must process as he speaks and therefore needs to hear himself talk. Under pressure he desires the ear of another, not for advice, but as a means of venting a frustration or problem. The Seller **loves people**, and yet because his Doer is lower would prefer that others initiated a relationship with him. Therefore, he is normally most comfortable in a position where people come to him. However, if emotionally starved or isolated, the Seller will readily seek out others' companionship. The Seller child will go to school with one goal: to keep track of his friends and enjoy the standing of being "popular," since that will bring many relationships his way. This **desire for popularity** can lead to an unhealthy adaptation to the crowd. Add to this the propensity to make impulsive decisions, and if the Seller were an automobile, his reverse gear would be worn out. He is a delight to be around, since the comfort of another is ever present in his wishes. However, those closest to him will have a tendency to feel abandoned when someone new enters the room and becomes the focus of the Seller. He is **optimistic, enthusiastic,** and quite adept at the art of **persuasion**. However, the Seller is also open to deception on three counts. First, he trusts nearly everyone and thinks (or rather feels) the best of others. Second, he has a natural ability to size up a person nonverbally simply by examining paralinguistic behaviors, reading people emotionally. This is a great asset until he misreads someone, and when he does, it is a major misread. Third, he has the habit of feeling and then acting upon that; this can reap great benefits and equally great regrets.

Biblical Character: Barnabas

MULTI-FACETED
Thinker/Doer/Feeler

The multi-faceted unique-self type is commonly called the "**Jack of all trades**." The Chinese jokingly would call this person "a man of many knives, not one overly sharp." However, the Multi-faceted comes by his title genuinely, because he has **multiple abilities**. This person is of vast value on any journey and in nearly every business

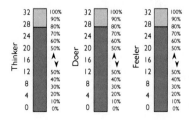

as the go-to person. He can be task oriented, a self-starter, and show empathy all in the span of one day. He is a **team** player, **loyal**, and quite enjoyable to be around, but is both an introvert and extrovert. Because of his ability to do many things, he can have difficulty focusing and will most likely approach settling on a lifelong career like the homing pigeon; he will **circle**, sometimes for years. Then something stirs and he knows the direction in which he must go. Expect the Multi-faceted to hold a variety of jobs in the course of his life. He is **balanced** and even-tempered, not easily given to anxiety, anger, or stress, because experience has proven to him that with time, the situation can be resolved. Do not expect him to commit quickly, desire to control others, or enjoy being controlled. When it comes to stress, he is not easily ruffled; there is a **pause**, a wait and see, and then he acts with the desire to do the right thing as he has surmised it. Therefore, it is important to give him time to process. In a disaster, he will be found calmly working, being quite adept at **problem solving**. There are downsides to the one with this temperament, since he can feel crazy because of the struggle between the temperament traits as they assert their particular leanings. In marriage, the spouse may not know what to expect on any given day, depending on the situation that has brought the Multi-Faceted's thinker, doer, or feeler to the fore. The Multi-faceted would prefer that affection be initiated toward him. Also, he craves a **model**, although a model for such a person is hard to come by. The other unique-self expressions will more easily find others with a like personality from whom to learn. For the multi-faceted child, **direction** is very important in the formative years. All in all, the person can best be described as a **Swiss Army Knife**.
Biblical Character: Onesimus

Important Information to Possess
When Raising a Family

Understanding the unique selves of our children should affect our prayer life and methods of instruction for them.

The child who is a Thinker will have the tendency to dwell on the negative; we need to pray that he will not spiral into depression, since Thinkers have the highest rate of suicide. He should be taught to set his mind on the things above (Philippians 4:6-8) and led to find a suitable vent for his internalized anger and frustration with the world and others. Disciplining the Thinker is usually a matter of reasoning and not allowing his negative attitude concerning the family, school, and world to continue.

The child who is a Doer needs prayer and development in the area of being sensitive to the needs and feelings of others. We can also create an environment wherein the child can find a godly vent for his creativity. The child will further need prayer concerning his natural tendency to submit to no authority, including God's. Indeed, of all the temperaments, discipline is the most arduous task when applied to the Doer. He will rarely respond to the threat of punishment or the promise of reward. Often corporal punishment is needed, for the Doer cannot see the damage done by his behavior.

If the child is a Feeler, then we must seek the Lord to give protection and wisdom, because the child will have the habit of following the morals of the crowd. Also, we will ask the Lord to decrease the child's subjectivity, which can lead to depression. The Feeler is the simplest of all temperaments to discipline, since he will respond to the threat of punishment and the method of reasoning. The one thing the Feeler dreads more than anything else is that his behavior has caused suffering for others.

To punish a child who is a muscle member, a Doer, by making him pick up the yard and mow the lawn is no punishment at all. To require the internal organ, the Thinker, who is given by nature to detail, to write his name a hundred times would not be punishment but a foretaste of heaven! On the other hand, to make the muscle member write something one hundred times, the internal organ work in the yard, or the sensory member stay off the phone and not socialize would truly be punishment!

Understanding the unique selves lessens our judgment of others and increases our enjoyment of the family of God.

Instructions for The Unique Self Test

The Unique Self Test is structured to give insight into the normal behavior of a Thinker, Doer, and Feeler in three areas: in a social environment, under stress, and with regard to the giving and receiving of affection.

Step 1

Simply answer each question by checking under the true or false column. Mark true if you agree with the statement about yourself, and mark false if you disagree.

Step 2

At the end of each section, score each separate area by doubling the number of "true" responses you gave.

Please note that a lower score does not indicate a problem! The test is merely measuring your highest unique-self trait. The higher the score, the more compulsive the trait. The lower the score, the less compulsive. If a score is very low (like around 10%), this can indicate masking of the unique-self trait.

Step 3

After completing all of the test, transfer the total score for each section to the scoring page, Box A's score in Box A, etc.

Helpful Hints on Answering Questions

1. Read the question once quickly.

2. Answer true or false (agree with the statement or disagree) on the basis of what you feel at least 51% of the time.

3. Answer with your initial response to the question.

4. If you cannot answer the question, you are allowed to leave one question unanswered on each section.

5. There is no right or wrong answer; the test only reflects your unique self. For example, there is nothing wrong with preferring to work with things rather than people.

6. If true and false is not making sense when attempting to answer, remember to think in terms of agree or disagree.

7. If it helps you to answer, insert your name where the word "I" appears. Example: "John" prefers to work with things rather than people.

PART 1 Section 1 – Box A

STATEMENT	TRUE	FALSE
I prefer to work with things rather than people.	☐	☒
I internalize my frustration with others.	☒	☐
I am often critical of myself.	☒	☐
People should keep the rules.	☒	☐
By the end of the day I feel tired.	☒	☐
People frustrate me.	☒	☐
I want others to invite me to events.	☐	☒
People are too inconsistent.	☒	☐
I do not like others inspecting my work or giving advice.	☒	☐
I want to know what will happen next.	☒	☐
I am always thinking.	☒	☐
I enjoy being alone.	☒	☐
It is hard for me to fall asleep immediately.	☒	☐
I want lots of information on the outcome before I act.	☒	☐
I dislike change.	☒	☐
I think of myself as analytical.	☒	☐

Total number of True answers	14
(Double the number of True answers)	14
TOTAL – Transfer to Box A	28

PART 1 Section 2 – Box B

STATEMENT	TRUE	FALSE
I want to be in control.	☒	☐
I like a challenge.	☒	☐
Rules are frustrating.	☐	☒
People are lazy.	☐	☒
I like it when others follow my plan.	☒	☐
I have lots of ideas much of the time.	☒	☐
I feel circumstances box me in.	☒	☐
People need to listen to me more.	☒	☐
Others lack the vision to help me accomplish my goals.	☒	☐
I prefer being the boss.	☒	☐
Problems challenge me.	☒	☐
Others often misunderstand me.	☒	☐
Others see me as harsh and uncaring.	☐	☒
When I get mad everyone knows it.	☐	☒
I like to see things happen immediately.	☐	☒
I hate routine.	☐	☒

Total number of True answers	10
(Double the number of True answers)	10
TOTAL – Transfer to Box B	20

PART 1 Section 3 – Box C

STATEMENT	TRUE	FALSE
I enjoy being with people.	☐	☒
I enjoy staying up late when I'm with others.	☐	☒
My feelings are easily hurt.	☐	☒
It bothers me if I hurt others.	☒	☐
I hate routine work.	☐	☒
I prefer to work with people and not be left alone.	☒	☐
I enjoy social activities.	☐	☒
I often feel as though others do not like me.	☐	☒
I do not like to be rejected.	☒	☐
I dislike being alone.	☐	☒
I like to motivate other people.	☒	☐
I cry easily.	☐	☒
I enjoy helping other people.	☒	☐
I like to include others in my projects.	☐	☒
I find myself easily influenced by others.	☐	☒
I like belonging to an organization.	☒	☐

Total number of True answers [6]
(Double the number of True answers) [6]
TOTAL – Transfer to Box C [12]

PART 2 Section 1 – Box D

STATEMENT	TRUE	FALSE
Under pressure I often withdraw.	☒	☐
I don't expect things to go well.	☐	☒
I discipline myself when troubled.	☒	☐
I analyze problems.	☒	☐
Under pressure I realize the faults of others.	☒	☐
I am soft-spoken if under pressure.	☐	☒
I often stay up late thinking when under stress.	☐	☒
I become critical when things are not going well.	☒	☐
I seek advice from others.	☒	☐
Stress yields too many decisions to make.	☒	☐
If I work harder I can fix the problem.	☒	☐
I don't want to make the same mistake twice.	☒	☐
I become agreeable under stress.	☐	☒
Others often let me down.	☒	☐
I can't seem to stop thinking about the problem.	☐	☒
Under stress I become introspective (self-analyzing).	☒	☐

Total number of True answers	11
(Double the number of True answers)	11
TOTAL – Transfer to Box D	22

PART 2 Section 2 – Box E

STATEMENT	TRUE	FALSE
Under pressure I immediately confront others.	☐	☒
Conflict does not bother me.	☐	☒
People are the main cause of problems.	☒	☐
I explode during conflict.	☐	☒
I want others to follow me.	☒	☐
I use others to fix a problem.	☒	☐
I must do something if under pressure.	☒	☐
Others should listen to my ideas.	☒	☐
Problems are a normal part of life.	☒	☐
I enjoy a good fight.	☐	☒
Waiting is difficult.	☒	☐
Never avoid a problem.	☐	☒
It shouldn't take long to fix a problem.	☐	☒
I cannot help out unless others will listen.	☐	☒
People have too much anxiety under pressure.	☐	☒
I believe others should lead, follow, or get out of the way.	☒	☐

Total number of True answers	8
(Double the number of True answers)	8
TOTAL – Transfer to Box E	16

PART 2 Section 3 – Box F

STATEMENT	TRUE	FALSE
I become depressed when things don't go well.	☑	☐
I persuade others to follow me.	☑	☐
I sell my ideas.	☑	☐
When in conflict I avoid others.	☑	☐
I will often shut down under pressure.	☑	☐
Life is not fair.	☑	☐
No one likes me when there is conflict.	☐	☑
Tomorrow is another day; things will be better.	☐	☑
I feel sorry for others.	☐	☑
It was just a matter of time before things went bad.	☐	☑
I need to talk through my problems.	☑	☐
I attack problems differently each day.	☑	☐
I want others to follow me.	☑	☐
I feel there is nothing I can do.	☐	☑
I worry.	☐	☑
I contact others so they'll listen.	☐	☑

Total number of True answers: 9

(Double the number of True answers): 9

TOTAL – Transfer to Box F: 18

PART 3 Section 1 – Box G

STATEMENT	TRUE	FALSE
I do not like being touched.	☒	☐
I easily remember past hurts.	☒	☐
I want those around me to be consistent.	☒	☐
I only want a few close friends.	☒	☐
I expect too much from those I love.	☐	☒
I have trouble communicating my expectations.	☐	☒
I stuff others' failures and won't mention them.	☒	☐
I don't want anyone talking to me until I'm ready.	☐	☒
I can't stand it when I'm lied to.	☒	☐
I have trouble remembering past hurts.	☐	☒
I don't understand why others want to be touched.	☐	☒
I like to be reassured that everything is all right.	☒	☐
I don't want others to think they know me.	☐	☒
I hold feelings in until I explode.	☒	☐
I'm too tired to talk at night.	☒	☐
I do not feel very affectionate.	☐	☒

Total number of True answers	9
(Double the number of True answers)	9
TOTAL – Transfer to Box G	18

PART 3 Section 2 – Box H

STATEMENT	TRUE	FALSE
Others are too easily offended.	☒	☐
I want to lead in relationships.	☐	☒
People should forgive and forget.	☐	☒
I don't like being shocked.	☒	☐
I don't want to analyze everything that is wrong.	☒	☐
I should be the final authority.	☐	☒
It is no big deal if someone is tardy.	☐	☒
I like to show love by planning fun activities.	☐	☒
Others don't make decisions quickly enough.	☐	☒
People are easily offended.	☒	☐
I don't always have time for everyone's emotional needs.	☒	☐
People want too much from me.	☒	☐
Those I love should not control me.	☒	☐
I can't understand the complaints about me.	☐	☒
I can expect others to let me down.	☒	☐
I don't mind raising my voice.	☐	☒

Total number of True answers	8
(Double the number of True answers)	8
TOTAL – Transfer to Box H	16

PART 3 Section 3 – Box I

STATEMENT	TRUE	FALSE
I want to be praised.	☒	☐
My desire is for others to notice my accomplishments.	☐	☒
People need to act like they love each other.	☒	☐
I like physical expressions of love.	☐	☒
I want others to answer me.	☒	☐
I dislike complex relationships.	☒	☐
I want to be held.	☐	☒
I desire popularity.	☐	☒
Forgiveness is easy.	☐	☒
I want as many friends as possible.	☐	☒
Sometimes I give up on others.	☒	☐
I enjoy verbal acceptance.	☐	☒
I like doing "big" things to make people happy.	☐	☒
Bad relationships can make me depressed.	☒	☐
I like being appreciated.	☒	☐
I want those around me to listen to me.	☒	☐

Total number of True answers	8
(Double the number of True answers)	8
TOTAL – Transfer to Box I	16

What to remember when
interpreting the test

The test is not a perfect representation of your personality. There are as many blends and variations as there are people. Typical blends have already been presented. The test interpretations are generalizations.

In each area—Social, Stress, and Affection—we are looking for the highest score. When scores are equal, it is often true to say the Doer trait will take dominance, followed by the Thinker and then Feeler.

After determining the percentage of each unique-self trait in each area, turn to the pages detailing the Thinker, Feeler, and Doer characteristics and mark those that apply to you. For example, if the percentage score is 50%, then mark the half of the descriptions pertinent to your particular unique self.

The test does not attempt to change what you are but merely reveal it. It is not a psychological test.

One goal is to allow us to view relationships and the world around us from the shoes of another. Turn back to page 46 to discover how this information affects the raising of children.

A SOCIAL ENVIRONMENT

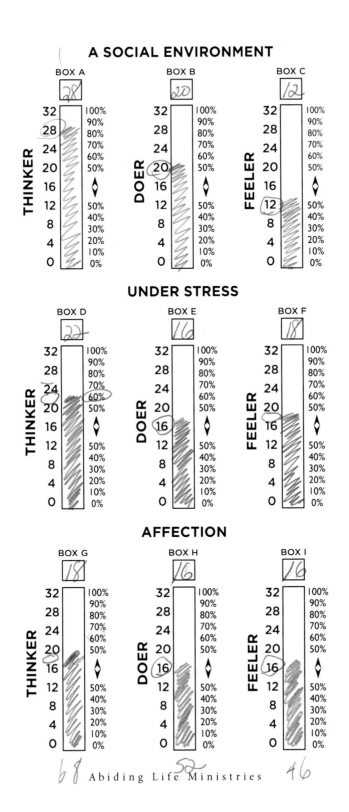

BOX A _28_

THINKER

32 — 100%
_28_ — 90%
— 80%
24 — 70%
— 60%
20 — 50%
16 — ◊
12 — 50%
8 — 40%
— 30%
4 — 20%
— 10%
0 — 0%

BOX B _20_

DOER

32 — 100%
— 90%
28 — 80%
— 70%
24 — 60%
_20_ — 50%
16 — ◊
12 — 50%
— 40%
8 — 30%
4 — 20%
— 10%
0 — 0%

BOX C _12_

FEELER

32 — 100%
— 90%
28 — 80%
— 70%
24 — 60%
20 — 50%
16 — ◊
_12_ — 50%
8 — 40%
— 30%
4 — 20%
— 10%
0 — 0%

UNDER STRESS

BOX D _22_

THINKER

32 — 100%
— 90%
28 — 80%
24 — 70%
— 60%
20 — 50%
16 — ◊
12 — 50%
8 — 40%
— 30%
4 — 20%
— 10%
0 — 0%

BOX E _16_

DOER

32 — 100%
— 90%
28 — 80%
24 — 70%
— 60%
20 — 50%
16 — ◊
12 — 50%
8 — 40%
— 30%
4 — 20%
— 10%
0 — 0%

BOX F _18_

FEELER

32 — 100%
— 90%
28 — 80%
24 — 70%
— 60%
20 — 50%
16 — ◊
12 — 50%
8 — 40%
— 30%
4 — 20%
— 10%
0 — 0%

AFFECTION

BOX G _18_

THINKER

32 — 100%
— 90%
28 — 80%
24 — 70%
— 60%
20 — 50%
16 — ◊
12 — 50%
8 — 40%
— 30%
4 — 20%
— 10%
0 — 0%

BOX H _16_

DOER

32 — 100%
— 90%
28 — 80%
24 — 70%
— 60%
20 — 50%
16 — ◊
12 — 50%
8 — 40%
— 30%
4 — 20%
— 10%
0 — 0%

BOX I _16_

FEELER

32 — 100%
— 90%
28 — 80%
24 — 70%
— 60%
20 — 50%
16 — ◊
12 — 50%
8 — 40%
— 30%
4 — 20%
— 10%
0 — 0%

_68_   _52_   _46_